Instant Ubuntu

Your complete guide to making the switch to Ubuntu

Christer Edwards

PUBLISHING

BIRMINGHAM - MUMBAI

Instant Ubuntu

First published: September 2013

Production Reference: 1230913

Published by Packt Publishing Ltd.
Livery Place
35 Livery Street
Birmingham B3 2PB, UK.

ISBN 978-1-78328-087-2

www.packtpub.com

Credits

Author

Christer Edwards

Reviewer

Goldin Evgeny

Acquisition Editors

Erol Staveley

Pramila Balan

Commissioning Editor

Poonam Jain

Technical Editor

Kapil Hemnani

Project Coordinator

Sherin Padayatty

Proofreader

Elinor Perry-Smith

Production Coordinator

Manu Joseph

Cover Work

Manu Joseph

Cover Image

Aditi Gajjar

About the Author

Christer Edwards began his career as a professional Linux instructor and avid technical blogger, publishing regular tutorials on using and improving Ubuntu systems. His love for teaching soon led him to a part-time instructor position at the University of Utah, where he has taught a variety of topics. In his day job, he currently works as a System Administrator for a large international company maintaining thousands of servers worldwide. He currently lives in Utah, where he enjoys exploring the outdoors.

I'd like to thank Casandra for her support in writing this book.

About the Reviewer

Goldin Evgeny is a veteran Java developer, starting with JVM bytecode instrumentation at IBM, and going all the way through enterprise application and web development at BMC and Thomson Reuters. He currently works as a build, automation, and release engineer.

www.packtpub.com

Support files, eBooks, discount offers and more

You might want to visit www.packtpub.com for support files and downloads related to your book.

Did you know that Packt offers eBook versions of every book published, with PDF and ePub files available? You can upgrade to the eBook version at www.packtpub.com and as a print book customer, you are entitled to a discount on the eBook copy. Get in touch with us at service@packtpub.com for more details.

At www.packtpub.com, you can also read a collection of free technical articles, sign up for a range of free newsletters and receive exclusive discounts and offers on Packt books and eBooks.

packtlib.packtpub.com

Do you need instant solutions to your IT questions? PacktLib is Packt's online digital book library. Here, you can access, read and search across Packt's entire library of books.

Why Subscribe?

- ✦ Fully searchable across every book published by Packt
- ✦ Copy and paste, print and bookmark content
- ✦ On demand and accessible via web browser

Free Access for Packt account holders

If you have an account with Packt at www.packtpub.com, you can use this to access PacktLib today and view nine entirely free books. Simply use your login credentials for immediate access.

Table of Contents

Instant Ubuntu   **1**

  So, what is Ubuntu?   **3**

  Installation   **5**

    Step 1 – download   6

    Step 2 – installer   7

    Step 3 – reboot   13

    And that's it!   13

  Quick start – desktop tour   **14**

    Launcher   14

    Ubuntu Dashboard   15

    Home Folder   16

    Firefox web browser   16

    LibreOffice Writer   17

    LibreOffice Calc   17

    LibreOffice Impress   17

    Ubuntu Software Center   18

    Ubuntu One   18

    System Settings   19

    Workspaces   20

    Trash   21

    Ubuntu status bar   21

    Network Manager   22

  Top 10 features you need to know about   **23**

    Accessibility   24

    Accessories   25

    Customization   26

    Games   28

Graphics   30
Internet   32
Media   34
Office   36
System   37
Software sources   38
A few extras   39
People and places you should get to know   **40**
Official sites   40
Community   40
Blogs   40
Twitter   40

Instant Ubuntu

Welcome to *Instant Ubuntu*. This book has been especially created to provide you with all the information that you need to set up Ubuntu. You will learn the basics of Ubuntu, get started using your new desktop, and discover some tips and tricks for using your new system.

This document contains the following sections:

+ *So, what is Ubuntu?* helps you find out what Ubuntu actually is, what you can do with it, and why it's so great.

+ *Installation* helps you learn how to download and install Ubuntu with the minimum fuss and then, set it up so that you can use it as soon as possible.

+ *Quick start – desktop tour* will give you a tour of the Ubuntu desktop and quickly show you where you can find the tools you need.

+ *Top 10 features you need to know about* helps you discover much of the software Ubuntu provides and learn how to use it. By the end of this section, you'll be able to get online, work with documents, and even play games!

+ *People and places you should get to know* provides you with many useful links to the project page and forums, as well as a number of helpful articles, tutorials, blogs, and the Twitter feeds of Ubuntu super-contributors.

So, what is Ubuntu?

Ubuntu is a free, open source operating system available for use on desktops, laptops, and servers. Since its initial release in 2004, Ubuntu has quickly become one of the most popular and widely used desktop Linux distributions in the world. Spend just a little time with Ubuntu and you'll discover why it is so widely adopted, and why its users are so passionate about using and sharing it.

At its core, Ubuntu is founded on the open source ideals of software freedom and accessibility. These fundamental principles are enshrined in the Ubuntu philosophy,

"We believe that every computer user":

- Should have the freedom to download, run, copy, distribute, study, share, change, and improve their software for any purpose, without paying licensing fees
- Should be able to use their software in the language of their choice
- Should be able to use all software regardless of disability

Ubuntu follows these principles by distributing only free software and allows users to improve upon the software as they see fit. This development model has allowed Ubuntu to grow by leaps and bounds in a short time. With new versions released twice each year, Ubuntu rapidly improves and refines all of its included software.

Every Ubuntu installation provides all the tools you need to be productive online or off. Whether it's web browsing and e-mail, or spreadsheets and presentations, Ubuntu provides a full suite of software out of the box.

- **Web browsing**: Ubuntu provides the award-winning Firefox web browser for secure and fast web browsing. Google Chrome and other free browsers are also available.
- **Social and e-mail**: Ubuntu makes communication with family and friends simple. With e-mail, instant messaging, micro-blogging, and video chat support available.
- **Productivity**: LibreOffice is an easy to use productivity suite designed to help you create professional documents, spreadsheets, and presentations. What's more, LibreOffice is also fully compatible with Microsoft Office.
- **Music and mobile**: Ubuntu is compatible with all of the common portable music players as well as Android and iPhone. Sync your music from your mobile device and listen to it using one of Ubuntu's available media players.
- **Photos and videos**: Ubuntu has great support for cameras and phones out of the box, and a long list of apps to help you manage, edit, and enjoy your photos and videos.

- **Software Center**: The Ubuntu Software Center is an integrated App store giving you access to thousands of free software applications at the click of a button. The Software Center will also handle all of the free security updates and software improvements.

Ubuntu is installed on millions of computers worldwide, providing a rich desktop experience for users everywhere. This book will not only help you install Ubuntu on your system, but give you an in-depth tour of the applications included.

Installation

This section will guide you through the steps required to install Ubuntu to your desktop system. We'll cover downloading the DVD image, burning the image to DVD, and finally, walk you through the actual installation. By the end of this section, you should have a running Ubuntu desktop!

Before we get to the actual installation, there are a few important items to address.

First, you'll want to make sure you have all the critical files backed up. Make sure you take the time to create backups of your pictures, documents, and other important files before you continue with the installation. These can be backed up to a DVD, external hard drive, or even a free cloud storage service, such as Dropbox.

Second, you'll need to determine which version and disk image is right for you. The Ubuntu download page offers a couple of options in terms of hardware support and release versions. Before you visit the download page, you'll want to consider the following information concerning Ubuntu releases:

A note about Ubuntu releases

Ubuntu is developed by a worldwide team of open source experts and free software enthusiasts. Using the open source model, Ubuntu is able to produce high-quality free software on a rapid six-month release cycle.

This rapid development cycle has allowed Ubuntu to produce eighteen releases in its first eight years. These releases are broken into two categories. **Long Term Support** (**LTS**) and **Development Releases**. The LTS releases, provided every two years, are the accumulation of the more fast-paced six-month development releases in between. This book is based on the LTS release, Version 12.04.

Ubuntu versions have two commonly used names. The development **codename** and the numeric release numbers. The development codename is decided upon early on in the release cycle, and takes the form of **Adjective Animal**. The numeric release numbers are the year and month that the version was released. Ubuntu Version 12.04, Precise Pangolin, on which this book is based, was released in April of 2012. Colloquially, Ubuntu releases are referred to by their development codenames. In this case, Ubuntu 12.04 "Precise Pangolin" is often referred to as simply **precise**.

Ubuntu releases a new version every six months, always in April and October, so you should expect new releases in October of 2012, April of 2013, and so on.

The second decision to make in regards to the download is whether to download the 32-bit or 64-bit version. Most hardware released in the past few years should be 64-bit compatible. The general rule of thumb is this, if you have more than 4 gigabytes of RAM in your machine, you'll likely want the 64-bit image. If you're unsure, the 32-bit image is the most compatible and is the safest option.

Step 1 – download

Ubuntu is distributed, free of charge, in the form of a downloadable DVD image. This image is available from the Ubuntu website at `http://ubuntu.com/download/desktop`. On this page, you can download either the latest development release or the latest LTS releases. I would suggest starting with the LTS release, Version 12.04, as this is the version that this book is based on.

The following screenshot is an example of the choice between the latest development release and the LTS release:

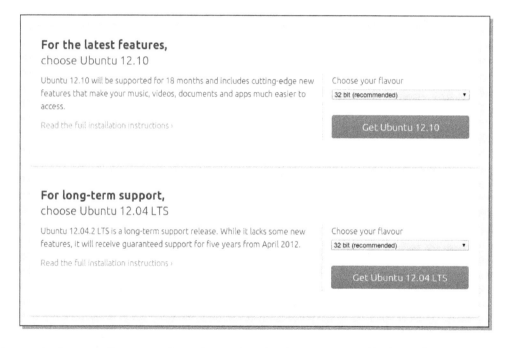

As seen in the preceding screenshot, Ubuntu downloads are separated by latest features against LTS. Also, notice the drop-down menu on the right side, allowing you to select the 32-bit or 64-bit versions. Select the release and 32-bit or 64-bit option best suited to your machine, and select **Get Ubuntu**.

The speed of your download will vary based on the speed of your Internet connection. While you're waiting for your download, you have a good opportunity to ensure you have everything backed up on your current system.

When your download is complete, use any DVD burning software to burn the image to a disk. These applications may vary based on your current operating system. Most new systems simply allow you to right-click on the Ubuntu `.iso file`, and select **Burn image to disk...**.

It is important that you use the option of burning the image to disk and not simply write the `.iso` as a file to the disk. The former will boot properly and load the installer, while the latter will simply create a file on the disk.

Step 2 – installer

The first screen you'll see during the installation is the **Welcome** screen. This screen allows you to select your preferred language and either **Try Ubuntu** or **Install Ubuntu**.

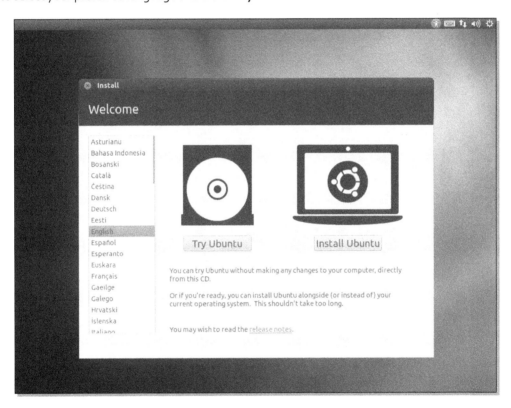

You can try Ubuntu without making any changes to your current running system, if you select **Try Ubuntu**. This option will launch a full Ubuntu desktop directly from the DVD and leave your current system intact. It should be noted that running the live system directly from the DVD will not be able to save any changes you make or maintain any settings changes across reboots. It also won't perform as well as it would, if it were installed on the hard disk. It is simply a method used for testing. I would suggest this method, if you're interested in taking a look at what Ubuntu has to offer before making the full commitment to installation.

When you're ready to install, select **Install Ubuntu,** and you'll be taken to the next step in the installation, **Preparing to install Ubuntu**.

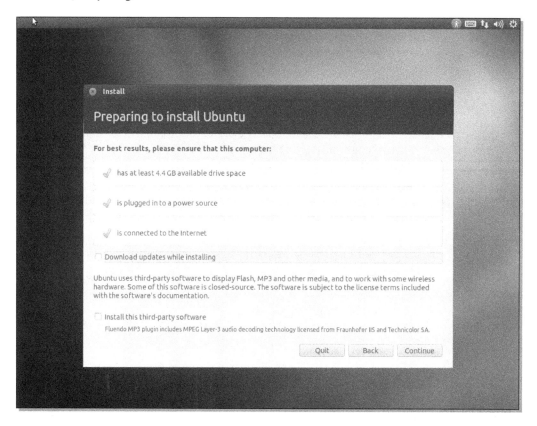

The second step in the installer ensures that you match the required hardware specifications. Ubuntu will run on a wide range of hardware, including some pretty old machines. This page checks to ensure that your computer:

- Has at least 4.4 GB available disk space
- Is plugged into a power source (primarily for laptops)
- Is connected to the Internet

The installer allows you to optionally select the option to **Download updates while installing,** and **Install this third-party software**. If you are connected to the Internet during your installation, I would recommend selecting these options.

The first will ensure that your fresh installation will be fully up-to-date upon completion. This means you'll have the latest security updates and patches the first time you boot up. The second will enable the ability to display Flash videos, listen to MP3s, and other media, and work with some types of proprietary wireless hardware.

When you've confirmed that you meet the minimum requirements and optionally selected the additional options, click on **Continue** to proceed to the next step.

The next screen, **Installation Type,** defines how the disk will be formatted and where Ubuntu should be installed. The two options seen here are to **Erase disk and install Ubuntu** or **Something else**. Depending on your current setup, you may see different options. It is possible to set up your machine in such a way that you can dual-boot both Windows and Ubuntu. The option to create or resize partitions manually is generally reserved for advanced users. Select that option if you're confident of what you're doing.

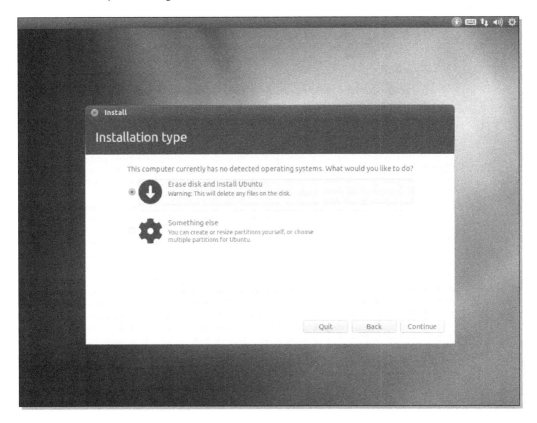

Basically, if you're ready to wipe out your current installation with Ubuntu, select the **Erase disk and install Ubuntu** option. If you'd like to dual-boot both Windows and Ubuntu, select that option. Again, select your preferred partitioning option, and click on **Continue**.

Once you've selected the installation type from the previous screen, you'll be given a chance to confirm those settings. In the following screenshot shown, the entire disk will be used. If you've selected a custom scheme or a dual-boot setup, you should see multiple partitions displayed in the main window. If you need to make any changes to your partitioning or disk setup, you can safely click on the **Back** button to return to the previous page.

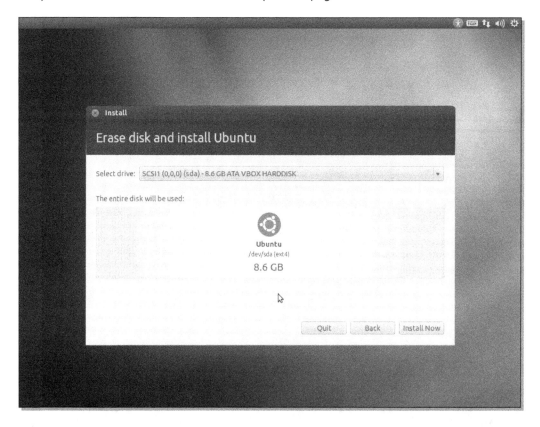

When you are ready to proceed with the installation, click on **Install Now**. This will proceed to make your selected changes to the disk, formatting, and partitioning where needed, and install Ubuntu to your system. This is the point of no return, so be sure you've made backups before continuing!

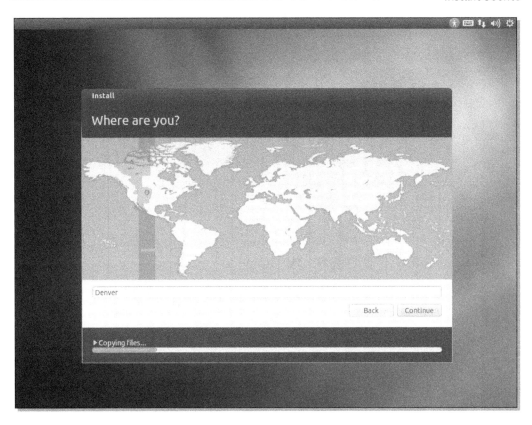

The Ubuntu installer will prompt you for more information while the main installation is now processing. The next screen displays a map of the world, cut into sections representing regional time zones. To select your local time zone, simply click on the appropriate region of the map. When you've selected the appropriate time zone, click on **Continue**.

The next item that the installer will prompt you for is the keyboard layout. The setting here will default to US English, but a wide range of keyboard layouts and variants are supported. If you use an alternate layout, select it here.

If you're unsure what your keyboard layout is, you can select the option to **Detect Keyboard Layout**, and be presented with a display of different characters. Simply press any matching character on your keyboard and the installer will detect your layout.

Once you've selected your preferred layout, click on **Continue** to proceed.

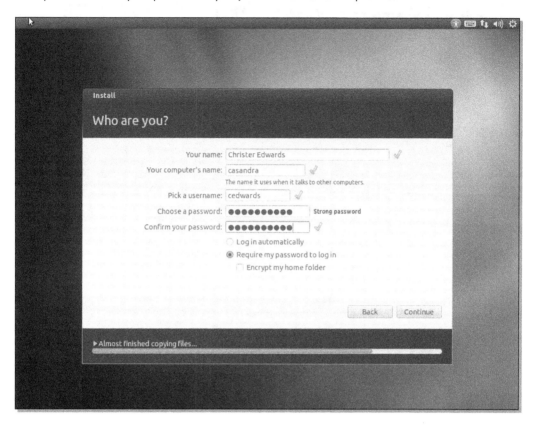

At this point, you're nearing the end of the installation and are prompted with information about your user. This information is important as it defines username and password to be used to log in to the machine. Be sure to make a mental note of the data you enter here.

First, enter your full name. Second, define a name for your computer to use when it communicates with other computers on the network. This name can be just about anything you like. Following that, you'll need to define your username and password. These values will be used to log in to your machine and secure your files. Be sure to select a strong, memorable password.

Once you've defined your username and password, you can toggle the setting to automatically login or require a password. For security reasons, it's suggested that you require a password to log in.

Finally, Ubuntu offers an encryption feature that will automatically encrypt files in your home folder. This will encrypt your documents, pictures, and other personal files against anyone that doesn't know your username and password. This setting is optional.

From this point on, the installer will run without further input from you. The last few screens are a slideshow of the features that you'll find once your Ubuntu installation is finished.

Step 3 – reboot

When the installer finishes the last of its tasks, you'll be prompted with a window to confirm that the installation is complete. In order to use your newly installed system, you'll need to reboot. Click on the **Restart Now** button to reboot into your newly installed Ubuntu system.

And that's it!

That's it! Surprisingly simple. You've now got a fresh Ubuntu installation ready to explore.

In the next section, we'll take a quick tour of your new system, and explore more of what an Ubuntu system has to offer. You'll learn how to get online, find and launch included applications, install new software, and more. This will be a quick overview with more details to follow in the following sections.

Quick start – desktop tour

Welcome to your new Ubuntu desktop! The aim of this section is to give you a brief overview of your new system, and a tour of Ubuntu's unique user interface. We'll outline where you can find and launch applications, give an overview of the Ubuntu launcher, get online, how to logout, reboot, shutdown, and change the basic settings. This is meant to be a basic overview of your new desktop environment. We'll go into greater detail in the next section.

At first glance, you'll notice that the desktop environment in Ubuntu is very likely different from what you might be used to. While that may be the case, I assure you the Ubuntu desktop environment is very user friendly, intuitive, and very customizable. Ubuntu has always focused on usability in their desktop environment, and the unique interface included in the Ubuntu desktop reflects that.

In the following pages, we'll explore the launcher, included applications, and status bar.

Launcher

The first thing you'll notice is that Ubuntu provides a launcher along the left side of the desktop. This launcher includes the most popular applications by default, and can be customized to include (or not include) just about anything you like. Feel free to explore the Ubuntu launcher by hovering your mouse over or right-clicking on any of the included icons. The following section will outline the default launcher applications, and their role in the Ubuntu desktop:

Ubuntu Dashboard

The first icon you'll encounter is the Ubuntu **Dashboard** launcher. This will launch the Ubuntu Dashboard, and allow quick searching of all your applications, files and folders, music, and videos. If you know the name of the application you're looking for, you can simply launch the Dashboard, type the application's name in the **Search Applications** field, and the Dashboard will find it for you. It also displays your recent applications, files, and downloads all on the main Dashboard screen.

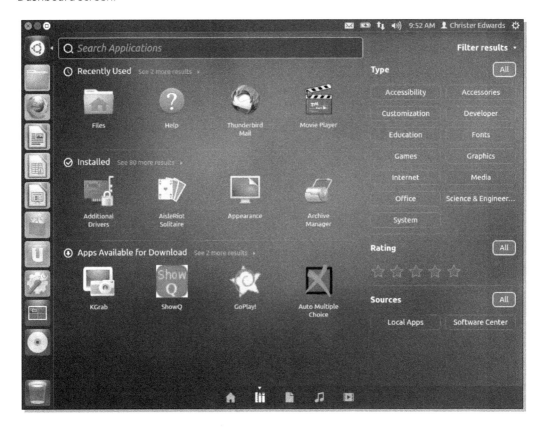

If you look toward the bottom side of the Dashboard display, you'll notice five icons. These icons represent the **Dashboard home**, **Applications**, **Files and Folders**, **Music**, and **Videos**. You can easily limit your searching and navigation, by filtering using these topics. In addition, each of the main sections within the Dashboard allows you to **Filter Results**, by clicking on the drop-down menu in the top-right corner of the Dashboard. This allows you to additionally filter results by a number of different categories. The results filter is also smart enough to filter based on different attributes depending on what tab you've selected. If you're on the **Music** tab, it will allow filtering by decade or genre. The **Files & Folders** tab will allow filtering by last modified date, type, or size. Select options as needed to narrow down your search results to find just the right match.

The Dashboard truly is a central place to quickly search for everything on your machine. You'll also notice that if you right-click on the **Dash** icon, it provides you with shortcuts to each of the key sections of the Dashboard: **Dashboard Home, Applications, Files and Folders, Music,** and **Videos**.

In addition to launching the Dashboard by selecting the icon, the Dashboard can also be launched using the Windows key on your keyboard, most modern systems now include a key with the Microsoft Windows logo, known as the Windows key. This is usually found to the left of the Space Bar key.

Home Folder

Second on the list of icons in the launcher is the **Home Folder** icon. This is a shortcut to your **Documents, Downloads, Music, Pictures,** and **Videos**. Home folder is the place for you to store and organize all of your files. Each user on an Ubuntu system will have their own Home folder to privately secure their files. Clicking on the **Home Folder** icon will launch Nautilus, the Ubuntu file browser, and default to home.

From here, you can explore your file system inside and outside of your **Home Folder** window. Just as we discovered with the Ubuntu **Dashboard** icon, right-clicking on the **Home Folder** icon will give you a shortcut list to each major section within your **Home Folder** window. It should be noted that while exploring files within Nautilus, you will only be able to edit files within your home folder, so feel free to look around. You won't be able to break anything, so don't worry.

Firefox web browser

You may recognize the next item in the launcher. Ubuntu comes out of the box with the hugely popular web browser, Firefox. Firefox is a fast, secure way to get online, and visit your favorite websites. Use Firefox to connect with friends and family, update your status online, and even safely play web-based games. In our modern Internet-connected era, a great web browser is a must-have, and Ubuntu provides one of the most popular in the base installation.

LibreOffice Writer

The next few applications in the launcher come from the highly-acclaimed productivity suite, LibreOffice. This Office suite provides you with a free word processor for writing and editing documents. LibreOffice Writer is intuitive, packed with features, and compatible with Microsoft Office formats. I'm even using LibreOffice right now to write this book! I'm sure you'll find LibreOffice Writer a perfect replacement for Microsoft Word.

We'll explore the LibreOffice productivity suite in more detail in the following section:

LibreOffice Calc

Ever need to work with spreadsheets? Ubuntu also provides the popular LibreOffice Calc application for managing spreadsheet data. This is another great replacement for the Microsoft Office suite that comes with Ubuntu out of the box, completely free. LibreOffice Calc provides you with all the powerful functionality of any standard spreadsheet application, and is always standard in every Ubuntu installation.

LibreOffice Impress

If you ever need to give presentations, LibreOffice Impress is the tool you'll want to use, a powerful presentation application designed to be compatible with the popular PowerPoint software. This tool will allow you to design amazing presentations for use at work or school.

Ubuntu Software Center

Next on the list is the Ubuntu Software Center. The Ubuntu Software Center is akin to an App Store, and includes tens of thousands of packages available for your Ubuntu system. If you'd like to install additional software on your system, simply launch the Ubuntu Software Center, search for your software, and click on **Install**. It's as easy as that!

The Ubuntu Software Center makes it easy to discover new applications as well. With a **What's New** and **Top Rated** section, the Ubuntu Software Center will give you an idea of the most popular applications available.

Most of the applications within the Ubuntu Software Center are free, and any that are not free are clearly marked. The Software Center is a centralized repository of free software applications allowing you to install any number of great applications with just a few clicks. This application will also handle all security updates and errata available for your system. You'll be notified of any available updates, and the Software Center will download and install them with your approval.

Ubuntu One

Ubuntu One is Ubuntu's free cloud storage offering. You can use Ubuntu One to safely store your files off-site, and automatically sync them between any machines tied to your Ubuntu One account. You can also get access to these files through your web browser from any machine connected to the Internet. Ubuntu One offers 5 GB of storage for free, and additional storage at affordable rates. This is a great place to safely archive important files. I use Ubuntu One cloud storage to store important documents and photos. I'm using Ubuntu One right now to store drafts of this book while I am writing it.

System Settings

Nearing the end of the list we have the **System Settings** application, which is a central place to customize all of your machine settings. This includes a wide range of available customization options for your machine, including **Appearance**, **Language Support**, **Keyboard Layout**, and **Privacy** settings. Also available are hardware support settings and system management tools, such as automatic backup utilities, accessibility, and user management. The **System Settings** application allows you to manage and customize a wide range of settings for your machine, all in one central place.

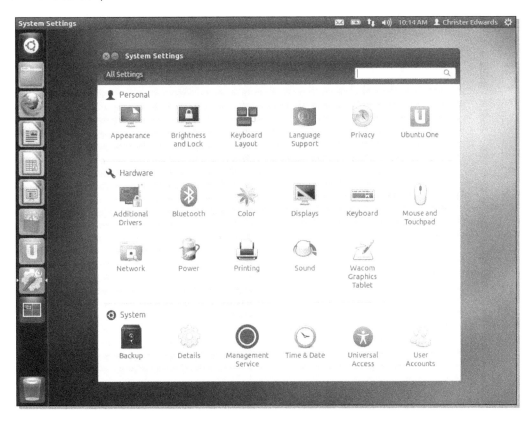

Workspaces

Ubuntu provides a very useful interface for managing multiple workspaces. This feature might be new to you, but I find it very helpful when managing multiple windows and applications. The workspaces interface allows you to manage multiple virtual workspaces, essentially allowing you to spread your applications out across multiple virtual desktop screens. I use this feature daily, and regularly switch between these virtual desktops to manage different applications.

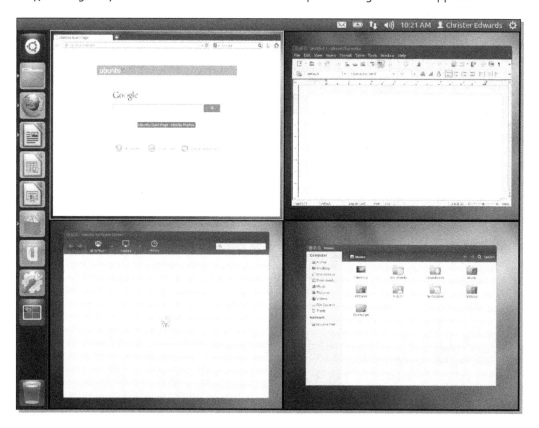

Admittedly, it may take a little bit of getting used to, but once you've got the hang of it, I'm sure you'll really appreciate the flexibility it gives you when running multiple applications at a time. Clicking on the **Workspaces** icon will zoom out of your current desktop workspace and give you a grid overview of four total workspaces. Simply double-clicking within any of these workspaces will zoom you back into that virtual desktop. This provides a very simple way to organize multiple windows and applications. For example, my common daily usage of my computer requires a **Terminal** console, a web browser, and an e-mail client. It is common to place each of these on their own workspace and dedicate a full screen to each application. You'll then be able to run applications in full screen, and simply switch between these workspaces to interact with each application. Switching workspaces can also be done using the keyboard shortcuts of *Ctrl + Alt* + arrow keys.

Trash

At the very bottom of the launcher bar, you'll discover an icon representing **Trash**. Any files you delete from your Ubuntu desktop will be placed in **Trash**, before they are permanently deleted. If you accidentally delete something, you'll also be able to recover it here.

Ubuntu status bar

The Ubuntu desktop provides a global menu bar across the top of the screen. This also includes a status area and a number of icons representing different aspects of your machine. A **battery** icon is included on laptops, network connection icon, sound and volume, clock, user status, and a shortcut to **System Settings,** and also a menu to allow you to logout, shutdown, or reboot your system. In the following screenshot, we see shortcuts to **System Settings..., Displays...,** and **Startup Applications....** There is also a notice letting you know that all software is up-to-date. This notice will change as security and other updates are made available. It will also notify you, if a system reboot is required.

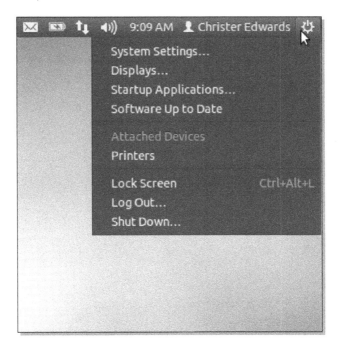

You'll also notice the **Lock Screen, Log Out...,** and **Shut Down...** buttons. As a tip, if you want to reboot your machine, you can click on the **Shut Down...** button, and it will give you an option to restart.

Network Manager

One last thing I'd like to cover before we wrap up this section is getting online. I'm sure you're ready to connect to the Internet and connect with friends on your favorite websites. The Ubuntu status bar provides an application to help you manage your network connectivity. This application is called **Network Manager**, and is a central place to manage wired and wireless networks. You'll notice headings for **Wired Network** and **Wireless Networks** as well as additional options for configuration and even VPN connections.

All you should need to do is select your preferred network from the available list and you'll be connected. If you're connecting to a wired network, Ubuntu should automatically connect during startup, and you'll see an icon that looks like an up and down arrow. This represents a connected wired network.

If you have specific network setting requirements you can select the **Edit Connections** option, and configure your network as needed. It includes the wired, wireless, mobile broadband, VPN, and DSL connection options.

You should now have a good idea of how to interact with your new Ubuntu desktop, where to find and launch applications, get online, and logout of your new system. In the following section, we'll cover these applications in more detail, go over the desktop customization, and install other popular software.

Top 10 features you need to know about

Now that you've had a basic tour of your new Ubuntu desktop, we're going to dig a little deeper and demonstrate some of the unique features that really makes Ubuntu stand out. We'll go over some of the previously outlined applications in more detail and delve deeper into the system settings to customize your system to meet your needs. We'll also demonstrate using the Ubuntu Software Center in more detail, by ensuring your system is fully up-to-date, install some popular applications, and suggest some tips for speeding-up parts of your system. By the end of this section, you'll be much more familiar with the power and flexibility of your Ubuntu desktop.

The following sections describe a number of the core applications, included in the base Ubuntu system as organized by category. You can view these categories, by launching Ubuntu Dash, selecting the **Applications** icon at the bottom of Dash, and using the **Filter results** option in the top-right corner. This will organize all of your installed applications by category, and allow you to explore them by similar type.

At different points during this section, you'll be prompted to install additional software to your system to improve on the included application set. Some of the suggested applications are only available after configuring the subscribed software sources at the end of this section. If you discover you're unable to find any of the suggested applications using the search feature of the Ubuntu Software Center, please see the *10 – Software Sources* section at the end of this section.

Accessibility

You might recall from the *So, what is Ubuntu?* section that Ubuntu is designed to be available and accessible to people around the world, despite any physical disabilities. This section will explore some of the accessibility options built into the Ubuntu system. The two main included applications are called **Onboard** and **Orca**.

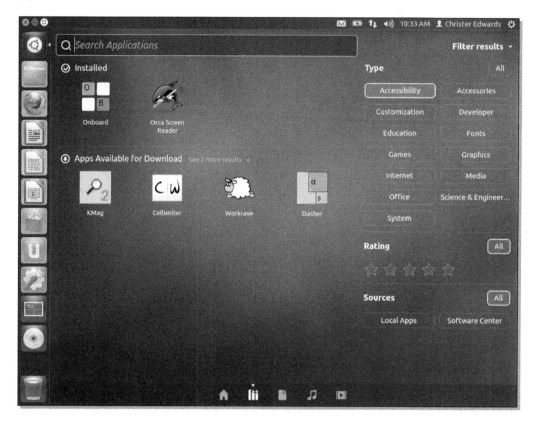

Onboard is an on-screen keyboard useful for tablet PCs and mobility-impaired users. This accessibility application allows users to use a virtual keyboard to type and interact with the machine. This is helpful for users who may be able to control a mouse, but are unable to fully operate a physical keyboard.

Orca is a free, open source, flexible, and extensible screen reader that provides access to the visual desktop via user customizable combinations of speech, braille, or magnification. This allows visually-impaired users the ability to interact with a visual desktop by allowing **Orca** to translate the visual information into speech or braille for them.

I have seen these applications in use by visually-impaired users, and it is very impressive how well they are able to interact with their machines despite these disabilities.

Accessories

Ubuntu provides a number of basic accessory utilities that provide the core functionality that you'd expect in a desktop operating system. These include applications, such as an archive manager, backup utility, calculator, and basic text editor. Here we'll introduce some of these applications to give you more of an idea of what you're able to do with your Ubuntu desktop.

Archive Manager is a very flexible utility for managing archived data. It supports a range of archive formats and provides you the ability to archive or unarchive data. This application supports archiving with the ZIP, TAR, RAR, and many other popular formats. If you've ever sent a ZIP file, this is the application you'll use to unzip it. If you need to create an archive, perhaps to create a manual backup of some of your data, you can use this application to archive and compress the data to be backed up elsewhere.

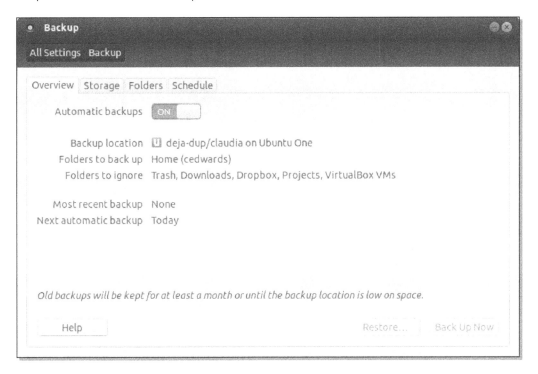

deja-dup is the included **Backup** utility. This application provides you with the ability to create automatic backups of your important files on a regular schedule. It supports daily, weekly, and monthly scheduling. The length of time to keep the backups is configurable, as well as the location of the backup. These backups can be automatically shared to cloud storage, FTP, Windows shares, or local-folder locations. With this application, there is no excuse to not have regular backups of your system!

The **Calculator** application is just what you'd expect at first look, a calculator. Upon closer inspection, you'll discover that it supports basic, advanced, financial, and programming modes of calculation. It's lightweight and easy to use, and of course, comes with Ubuntu out of the box.

Text Editor is a very flexible utility for everything from taking simple notes to creating computer programs. It isn't a full-blown word processor, but a plain-text text editor. I use **Text Editor** when I teach beginner programming courses at my local university, as it is flexible enough to support basic programming syntax, while still being simple enough for beginners to use. If you find that you need a basic editor to simply take notes for class, **Text Editor** is a great place to get started.

Customization

You'll discover that your Ubuntu desktop is very customizable, allowing you to make your desktop environment your own. You're able to customize the overall theme, desktop backgrounds, fonts, launcher characteristics, and much more. This section will outline a few of the basic things you might want to customize as you're getting started. This will include desktop look and feel, online account configuration, and even hardware and driver support.

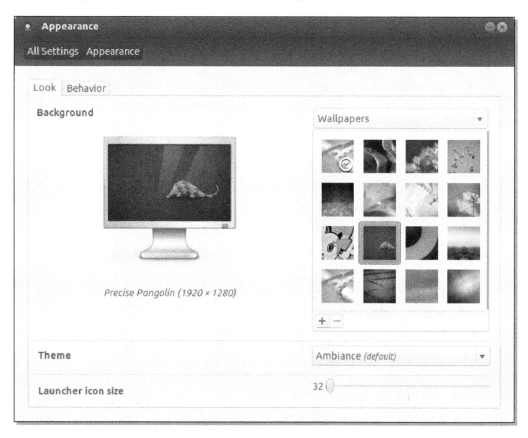

Customizing the look and feel of your Ubuntu desktop is done within the **Appearance** application. Here you'll be able to customize the desktop background, theme, and launcher settings. Select from the many included desktop wallpaper backgrounds and see a preview on the virtual display. Change your theme within the theme drop-down menu. You can also optionally customize the launcher icon size and overall behavior.

The default theme is called **Ambiance**. This provides the darker look that you see now. If you prefer a lighter theme, you might try the **Radiance** theme, which is an opposite look and feel to Ambiance. I like to configure my desktop with **Ambiance**, relatively small launcher icons, and an auto-hiding bar.

Feel free to customize your desktop however you like. Experiment with different themes and settings until you find the look and feel you prefer.

In regards to hardware support, Ubuntu provides a system to check for and install the drivers for proprietary hardware. This generally includes popular video cards from ATI or NVIDIA as well as some wireless network cards. While these drivers are not open source, Ubuntu can automatically detect the need for them, and handle the installation for you. This will give you better support for hardware not normally supported by open source operating systems. Launch the **Additional Drivers** menu item, and let Ubuntu scan your hardware. If it detects a need for proprietary drivers, it will prompt you, and walk you through the installation. If nothing is found, it simply means that you are already using open source drivers, and that your hardware is already fully supported.

Also available within the customization section is the **Broadcast Accounts** and **Broadcast Settings** applications. This is where you can configure your Twitter and Facebook chat accounts as well as preferences. Once configured, these accounts will be available directly from the status bar in the top right of your screen. If you click on the icon that looks like an envelope, you should see an entry for broadcast. This is where the broadcast accounts are integrated into your Ubuntu system, allowing you to update your status, and view and reply to messages from friends and family without needing to keep Facebook or Twitter open in a web browser.

Games

Ubuntu has both basic and more advanced gaming options available. Some of the games are things you'd expect, such as **Solitaire** or **Minesweeper**. Also included are tile-matching game **Mahjongg** and the number puzzle **Sudoku**. These are sure to provide hours of gaming fun. If you're interested in other gaming options, quite a few more are available in the Ubuntu Software Center.

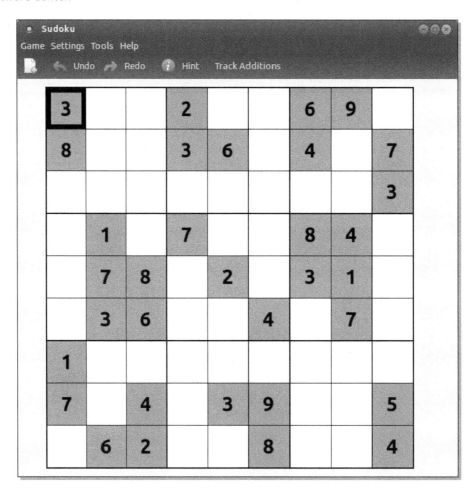

For those that are looking for gaming options beyond what is in the Ubuntu Software Center, Ubuntu is also supported by the Steam gaming platform. Historically, Steam has only supported Windows and Apple; however, Ubuntu was selected as the first (and currently only) Linux platform to be officially supported by Steam.

The following section will describe how to install Steam on your Ubuntu system and gain access to the Steam supported games for Ubuntu.

First, launch the Ubuntu Software Center and search for Steam in the search window. This should provide a number of results. You'll want to select the one labeled **The ultimate entertainment platform**. Select this option from the list, and click on **Buy**. You'll be prompted with and need to agree to the **Software License Agreement**. This will take you to the Ubuntu single sign-on page, where you'll need to log in or create a new account. If you have not yet registered for an Ubuntu account, you'll need to register here. This takes only a few minutes, and is completely free. Once you have created and/or logged into your account, the installation will continue.

When the installation is finished, a window will appear notifying you that you'll need to **Start Steam** to complete the installation. Click on **Start Steam** to continue. This will be followed by a **Steam Installation Agreement**, which you'll need to agree to. Check the box **I have read and accept the terms**, and click on **OK**. At this point, Steam will launch and begin downloading any available Steam updates. This may take a few minutes depending on your Internet connection.

From this point, you'll have the option to create a new Steam account or sign into an existing account. If you've played Steam games on other platforms, you should be able to use your existing credentials here. If you're new to Steam and want to get started, create a new account, and continue.

From here on you're ready to play Steam games!

Graphics

Your new Ubuntu system includes some very helpful applications in terms of graphics management and editing. You'll find the basic photo viewer applications, PDF viewers, basic graphic editing software, and even more advanced full editing suites available in the Ubuntu Software Center. Here we'll explore some of the offerings available, and outline how to install GIMP, the free software-equivalent to Adobe's Photoshop.

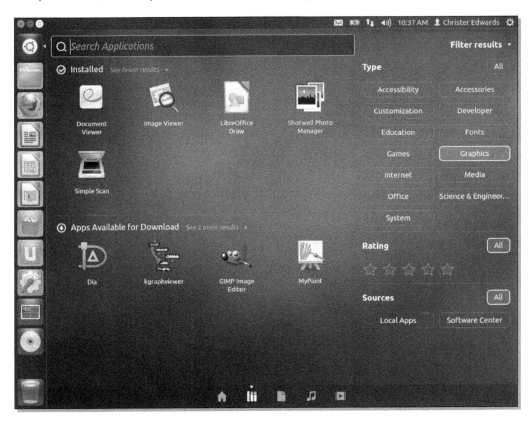

For basic photo viewing, you have a couple of options available. First, there is the **Document Viewer** and **Image Viewer** applications, which are applications used when viewing documents and photos in a read-only format. You won't be able to do any editing with these, but they're perfect for simply browsing your documents or photos, and displaying what you currently have.

If you need something more, you'll find the **Shotwell Photo Manager** available also. This application allows for basic rotation, cropping, red-eye reduction, basic image enhancements, and more. It isn't a full-blown Adobe Photoshop equivalent, but if all you're doing is some basic cropping and touch-up of photos imported from your digital camera, it likely has all the options you need. I used the **Shotwell Photo Manager** to crop and edit the screenshots used in this book.

If you are of the type that wants to do even more with your photos, you'll likely want the **GIMP Image Editor** application. **GIMP** stands for **GNU Image Manipulation Program**, and is the free software solution to the proprietary Photoshop application. GIMP supports most of the same features of Photoshop and is available in the Ubuntu Software Center. The following section will describe how to install GIMP and start using it on your Ubuntu system.

I'm sure at this point, you're one step ahead of me in knowing you'll need to navigate to the Ubuntu Software Center. From there you can search for GIMP in the search field, and look for the listing for **Create images and edit photographs**. Click on **Install**, and enter your administrative password when prompted. If you're interested, there are also add-ons available for GIMP that should be presented to you below the main description within the Ubuntu Software Center. These include the following add-ons:

- An extra set of brushes, palettes, and gradients for GIMP
- Scanner plugin for GIMP
- The GIMP plugin for GREYC's Magic Image Converter
- Print plugin for GIMP
- Repository of optional extensions for GIMP
- Userspace virtual file system backends
- The command-line tools for extracting data for the XCF files

These are all optional of course, and you may not need them until you get into some of the more advanced features of GIMP, but it's good to know that they're available.

Internet

Within the Internet section of the Ubuntu Dash, there are a number of options available for getting online and connecting with friends, family, and co-workers. From Internet browsing to e-mail to Twitter and Facebook, Ubuntu provides some of the best applications in terms of Internet connectivity. We'll start here with the web browser Firefox, outline how to install the Chrome browser, and start checking e-mail with Thunderbird. There are of course, a number of additional Internet-related applications available in the Ubuntu Software Center, but there are too many to mention here.

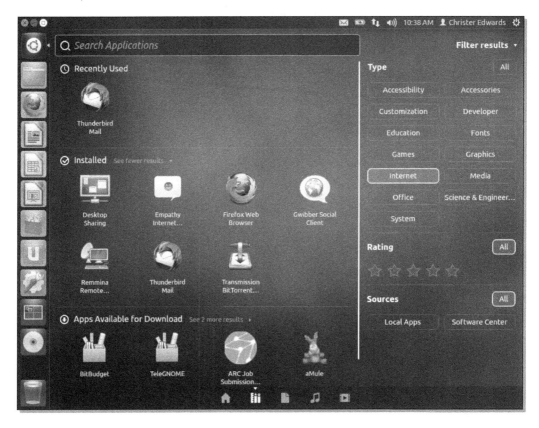

We'll begin with Firefox, one of the most popular, secure, and extensible Internet browsers available today. Firefox is included in the default installation and should be one of the default applications included in the launcher bar. If you haven't already, go ahead and launch Firefox, and get online. Browse to your favorite websites, post an update on a social media site about your new system, or share a link to this book with your friends. I'm sure they'll enjoy exploring Ubuntu as much as you do!

Firefox has a number of configuration options available and is extensible through the included add-ons and extensions system. The extensions and add-ons are too many to number here, but we can take a minute and look at some of the configuration options.

To begin, open Firefox using the launcher, and open the **Preferences** menu. This can be found at **Edit | Preferences** in the **File** menu. The **Preferences** menu allows you to customize different aspects of your browsing experience, such as default home page, tab handling, privacy, security, and more. The default settings are generally pretty sane, but there are a couple of options that I generally like to change. First, under the **Privacy** tab, I check the box **Tell websites I do not want to be tracked**. This option disallows certain types of cookies often used by online advertisers to target or retarget advertising based on sites that you've visited or products you've viewed previously.

Toggling this setting is completely optional. This same tab also allows you to toggle what Firefox remembers about your browsing history. Customize this and other options as desired, and click on **Close**.

To install add-ons, navigate to the **Tools | Add-ons** option within the **File** menu, and you'll be taken to a page displaying your current **Add-ons**, **Extensions**, **Appearance**, **Plugin**, and **Language** options. You can quickly search for add-ons and extensions using the search bar at the top-right corner. Again, there are simply too many to mention here, but you can get an idea of what extensions are popular and available, by visiting `http://addons.mozilla.org`.

The Google Chrome browser is Google's alternative to Firefox, which is also available for Ubuntu systems. While not included in the default installation, it is available for download from the Google website at `http://google.com/chrome`. Visit this page, click on **Download Chrome**, and select the version to match your system. Currently Chrome formally supports the Ubuntu, Debian, openSUSE, and Fedora Linux distributions. You'll of course want to select the Ubuntu offering, and depending on your system, the 32-bit or 64-bit option. If you remember the *Installation* section, we discussed the differences between 32-bit and 64-bit. Select the same option here that you did at the *Installation* section, and click on **Accept and Install**.

Note: if you don't recall which option you selected, it's safe to select either. If it is incompatible with the rest of your installed system, you should be prompted accordingly, and you can simply go back and select the other option.

You should next be prompted with a window to **Open with** or **Save As**. You can safely save as and the Google Chrome installer will be saved to your `Downloads` folder. You can then find this file by navigating to `Downloads` within the Nautilus file browser, and double-click on the Google Chrome `.deb` file. This will open the Ubuntu Software Center and walk you through the rest of the installation. You'll likely be prompted for your administrator password somewhere along the way. Enter your credentials as needed, and within a couple of minutes the Google Chrome browser will be installed on your machine.

If you're wondering which browser you should use, it is completely up to you. I prefer the Google Chrome browser, but Firefox is a very worthy competitor. It really just comes down to personal preference, as both are considered very secure, support extensions, and are faster than most other browsers today.

Now that we've explored both Firefox and Google Chrome as web browsers, let's look at what Ubuntu has to offer in terms of e-mail management.

Thunderbird is included in the base installation of Ubuntu and is designed by the same people that make Firefox, the Mozilla foundation. This makes Thunderbird a very popular, secure, and fast solution for e-mail management that also supports similar extension architecture with the web browser. Here I'll briefly outline getting started with Thunderbird to download and manage your e-mail on your local system.

Thunderbird is not included in the launcher bar by default, so you'll need to search for it in the Ubuntu Dash, or select it from the filtered results within the applications section.

When you first launch Thunderbird, you'll be prompted with a getting started wizard to help you configure your e-mail account. Thunderbird includes a database of common e-mail providers around the world and their respective configuration options. This means all you should need to do is enter your e-mail address and password, and Thunderbird will do the rest. The more popular your e-mail provider, the better luck you'll have with this system. If you find that Thunderbird is unable to auto-detect your settings, you may need to contact your Internet service provider for additional details.

Once you have Thunderbird configured, you'll be able to send and receive e-mail from the application, quickly and easily. Thunderbird also supports features, such as spam filtering, and automatically organizing e-mail using filters and folders.

Media

Ubuntu comes with a great media player called Rhythmbox. This player has great support for a number of media formats, supports podcasts, last.fm integration, and connectivity to the Ubuntu One Music Store. Rhythmbox includes a very easy to use interface, allowing you to easily find and organize all of your music.

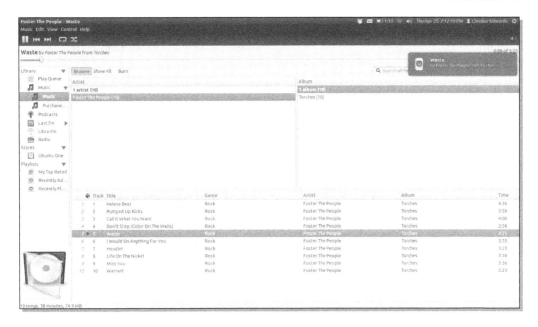

Rhythmbox supports the creation and importing of playlists, fetching of album art, search, and Internet radio. Rhythmbox is a preferred application for handling music collections.

When it comes to watching videos on Ubuntu, one player reigns supreme in supporting the widest number of formats and including the most features. This player is VLC. Unfortunately, VLC isn't installed by default on Ubuntu so we'll have to grab it from the Ubuntu Software Center. We can do that by launching the Software Center, and searching for VLC. You should see a result for **VLC Media Player: Read, capture, and broadcast your multimedia streams**. Select this from the list and then click on **Install**. As is the case any time you install software, you'll be prompted for your password, and then the installation will begin.

Once VLC is installed, you can make it the default application for different media types by launching the **System Settings** application, and selecting the **Details** option within the **System** section. This application gives you an overview of your system, allow you to set default applications, and configure the default action for removable media. Select the **Default Applications**, look for **Video** on the right side, and select **VLC** from the drop-down menu.

Office

As outlined in the previous section, Ubuntu provides the LibreOffice productivity suite in the default installation. This includes the Writer, Calc, Draw, and Impress applications. If you use your computer for school or work, these applications are probably something you'll use regularly. Whether you're writing papers or reports, managing spreadsheets, or creating detailed presentations, the LibreOffice suite has you covered.

LibreOffice Writer is flexible enough to take simple notes or write papers and books. I'm using Writer right now to write this book. There are far too many features to go into in much detail, but Writer is a very powerful, compatible word processor. It supports a number of document formats including the global Open Document Format standard. It can read and write Microsoft Office document formats as well as export directly to PDF or HTML.

LibreOffice Calc is the included spreadsheet application. This supports the same level of compatibility with other platforms and the features that you'd expect from any mature spreadsheet management application. I use LibreOffice Calc for everything from managing consulting services invoices to basic budgeting and fitness tracking. Calc is very intuitive for new users, while remaining powerful enough for professional data miners and number crunchers.

Impress is an outstanding tool for effectively creating multimedia presentations for work or school. These presentations can be enhanced using 2D and 3D clip art, special effects and transitions, animations, and even drawing tools. I have seen some very impressive presentations created with LibreOffice Impress. What's more, it supports the popular PowerPoint format and can even output directly to the Flash format for viewing online.

System

Last in the Dash is the **System** category. This category provides you with the system management tools you'd expect in any mature desktop environment. This section includes privacy settings, system monitors, system settings, and the update manager.

As you continue to use the Dash, you may notice that Ubuntu keeps track of your recently used applications, files, and folders. This can be configured within the **Privacy** settings. The options allow for limiting activity recording to specific files, folders, and even per-application. You also have the ability to erase the recorded history in the same way you might within a web browser. If you're concerned about privacy, you might elect to disable activity recording. It should be noted that all information recorded is completely anonymous, and is generally only used to offer you improved access to your recently used applications, files, and folders. The important thing to note is that your privacy is up to you, and can be configured all in one place.

System Monitor is a central overview of your system, process, resources, and disk usage.

From the **System** tab you're able to determine whether you've installed 32-bit or 64-bit Ubuntu, your Ubuntu version, kernel release hardware, and disk usage.

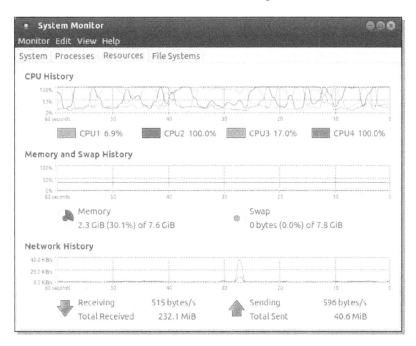

The **Processes** tab displays the processes currently running on your system and allows you to manage them. By right-clicking on the process you're able to stop, kill, end, and change process priority on most of the running applications on your system. This tab gives you a good overview of what is running and what may be using more than its share of CPU or memory.

The **Resources** tab gives you a visual overview of CPU history, memory and swap, and network history.

Finally, the **File System** tab gives you an overview of free and available disk space.

Software sources

The **Update Manager** is the application that handles all security and errata updates for you. It is likely that Ubuntu has made security and errata updates available for your installation and these will be presented by the **Update Manager** application. The following section will outline how to configure the update manager to check frequency, what sources you'd like to subscribe to, and even what location you'd like to download updates from.

The first thing the **Update Manager** application will do when launched is make sure your machine is fully up-to-date with security updates and errata. This will ensure that you have the latest security fixes applied and the latest improvements available for your version of Ubuntu. When you first launch the **Update Manager** application, you may be presented with a list of available updates. Before we apply these updates, I'd recommend making a few configuration changes to the **Update Manager** settings that will provide you with additional available packages and speed up the time it takes to check for and download updates.

First, open the **Update Manager** application from the Dash and click on the **Settings...** button on the bottom-left corner. This configuration section allows you to customize what you want to make available from the Software Center and even where you'd like to download it. Ubuntu provides mirrors of the software repositories all over the world. Selecting one closest to you can significantly improve your download speeds.

In the first section under **Ubuntu Software**, you'll see **Downloadable from the Internet**. I would suggest ensuring that the first four boxes are checked. Also, unless you're going to be developing Ubuntu software, you can safely uncheck the fifth box labeled **Source Code**. Next, select **Download from:** from the drop-down menu. This list should be populated with options to use the main server, the server for your country, or **Other...**.

Selecting the server for your country instead of the main server will offer some improvement, but you might also want to try the **Other...** option. This option will display a second menu allowing you to select a server in nearly any country around the world. There is also an option to try and determine the fastest server for your connection. If you click on **Select Best Server**, a series of tests will be performed to find the best mirror for your location. This can take a few minutes and will auto-select a location when it is finished. This test isn't always perfectly accurate. You might experiment with a few different locations until you find one that you feel performs the best.

The other items you might configure on this page are in the **Updates** tab. Here you can configure what types of updates you'd like to see and how often. If you're using the LTS release, you'll probably want the **Important**, **Recommended**, and **Unsupported** updates. Pre-release updates are for those who want to help test the updates before they're pushed to the rest of the public. Beware, while this will provide you with updates before everyone else, some can cause problems as they still need to be tested.

You're also able to update the frequency of which Ubuntu checks for security and errata updates. You can check for updates daily, every other day, weekly, or every few weeks. You can configure how Ubuntu will act when it finds available updates, including download, and install them automatically. I am a bit compulsive about my security and errata updates. I always like to have the latest and greatest software, which is why I have my system check for updates daily, automatically download and install them, and display a notification immediately when found. Of course, you don't have to use the same settings, but choose the right combination for you and your system.

Once you make these changes, Ubuntu will ask you for your administrative password, and then refresh against the server you selected. The **Update Manager** application may then have updates available, which you can apply by clicking on **Install Updates**.

A few extras

There are certain software packages that due to licensing restrictions, cannot be distributed with the Ubuntu CD, but are available through the Ubuntu Software Center. These packages include MP3 support, Flash media player, DVD playback, and more. As I'm sure you'll want support for these things on your Ubuntu system, this section outlines how to install them. The instructions here depend on having enabled the software sources in the previous section.

To install support for these formats, open the Ubuntu Software Center, and search for `ubuntu-restricted-extras`. This should come up with one result with the description of commonly used applications with restricted copyright (MP3, AVI, MPEG, TrueType, Java, Flash, Codecs). Select the result from the list, and click on **Install** on the right side of the window. You may be prompted to reboot for these changes to fully take effect. Once these are installed, you should now have full support for MP3 playback, Flash media player-based websites, and DVD playback.

People and places you should get to know

Ubuntu is easily the most user-friendly Linux distribution, specifically designed to be intuitive and welcoming to new users. While you're sure to have an easier time using Ubuntu as compared to many other Linux distributions available, there will come a point where you'll run into some difficulty in using your system and need some guidance. When that time comes, there are a number of online resources to help you along the way. This section introduces a number of these resources where you can find answers, read documentation, chat and meet with other users, and hopefully find the answers you need.

Official sites

- Homepage: http://ubuntu.com
- Official documentation: http://docs.ubuntu.com
- Community Wiki: https://wiki.ubuntu.com
- Official forums: http://ubuntuforums.org

Community

- Ask Ubuntu, a community driven Q&A site: http://askubuntu.com
- Keep up on the latest Ubuntu development news on the Fridge: http://fridge.ubuntu.com
- An aggregation of core Ubuntu contributors and developers: http://planet.ubuntu.com
- Local Community Support Teams: https://wiki.ubuntu.com/LoCoTeams

Blogs

- Ubuntu founder's blog: http://www.markshuttleworth.com/
- The blog of Jono Bacon, Ubuntu's community manager: http://www.jonobacon.org/blog/
- Ubuntu News, Apps, Reviews, and Features: http://omgubuntu.co.uk

Twitter

- Official Twitter Account for Ubuntu: https://twitter.com/ubuntu
- OMG Ubuntu! on Twitter: https://twitter.com/omgubuntu
- Jono Bacon on Twitter: https://twitter.com/jonobacon
- For more open source information, follow Packt at http://twitter.com/#!/packtsopensource

Thank you for buying
Instant Ubuntu

About Packt Publishing

Packt, pronounced 'packed', published its first book "*Mastering phpMyAdmin for Effective MySQL Management*" in April 2004 and subsequently continued to specialize in publishing highly focused books on specific technologies and solutions.

Our books and publications share the experiences of your fellow IT professionals in adapting and customizing today's systems, applications, and frameworks. Our solution based books give you the knowledge and power to customize the software and technologies you're using to get the job done. Packt books are more specific and less general than the IT books you have seen in the past. Our unique business model allows us to bring you more focused information, giving you more of what you need to know, and less of what you don't.

Packt is a modern, yet unique publishing company, which focuses on producing quality, cutting-edge books for communities of developers, administrators, and newbies alike. For more information, please visit our website: www.packtpub.com.

Writing for Packt

We welcome all inquiries from people who are interested in authoring. Book proposals should be sent to author@packtpub.com. If your book idea is still at an early stage and you would like to discuss it first before writing a formal book proposal, contact us; one of our commissioning editors will get in touch with you.

We're not just looking for published authors; if you have strong technical skills but no writing experience, our experienced editors can help you develop a writing career, or simply get some additional reward for your expertise.

Learning Nagios 3.0

ISBN: 978-1-847195-18-0   Paperback: 316 pages

A detailed tutorial to setting up, configuring, and managing this easy and effective system monitoring software

1. Secure and monitor your network system with open-source Nagios version 3

2. Set up, configure, and manage the latest version of Nagios

3. In-depth coverage for both beginners and advanced users

Linux Shell Scripting Cookbook

ISBN: 978-1-849513-76-0   Paperback: 360 pages

Solve real-world shell scripting problems with over 110 simple but incredibly effective recipes

1. Master the art of crafting one-liner command sequence to perform tasks such as text processing, digging data from files, and lot more

2. Practical problem solving techniques adherent to the latest Linux platform

3. Packed with easy-to-follow examples to exercise all the features of the Linux shell scripting language

Please check **www.PacktPub.com** for information on our titles

www.ingramcontent.com/pod-product-compliance
Lightning Source LLC
LaVergne TN
LVHW081349050326
832903LV00024B/1375